THE CYCLE THAT BROKE

*Breaking Generational and
Spiritual Strongholds*

DR. NATASHA BIBBINS

The Cycle That Broke: Breaking Generational and Spiritual Strongholds

© November 2025

By Dr. Natasha Bibbins

Published in the United States of America by

ChosenButterflyPublishing LLC

ChosenButterfly
PUBLISHING

www.ChosenButterflyPublishing.com

ISBN: 978-1-945377-57-0

First Edition Printing

Printed in the United States of America

November 2025

CONTENTS

PREFACE

Why Is Deliverance Important?

Deliverance is important because it gets to the root of the cycle—not just the symptoms. You can change behaviors, read self-help books, and set new goals, but without deliverance, the spiritual chains remain. Deliverance breaks the unseen agreements we've made with fear, rejection, addiction, pride, and generational curses. It exposes the enemy's grip and reclaims the territory of your soul. True freedom doesn't come from willpower—it comes from the power of God. Deliverance clears the spiritual clutter, allowing you to walk in clarity, purpose, and wholeness. It's not just about casting something out; it's about welcoming the presence of God in. Without deliverance, cycles may pause—but with deliverance, they are destroyed at the root.

Deliverance doesn't just manage the cycle—it demolishes it. While therapy addresses the mind and healing soothes the heart, deliverance goes after the spirit. It confronts the demonic strongholds, generational curses, and soul ties that quietly govern behaviors, emotions, and patterns. Many people try to fix cycles with willpower, routines, or even religion; however, this becomes a failed attempt because without the Spirit of God breaking the yoke, you will stay bound beneath the surface. Deliverance is not just shouting or laying hands—it's divine authority in action. It is heaven's intervention on Earth.

When you undergo *true* deliverance, you're not just free from something—you're *FREE* from *some things*. You're delivered from bondage, yes, but also delivered into destiny. Just think about that for one moment—if you have ever ordered a package but it has to go through a process before it can reach your address or its destination. You are that package. You have been ordered to take your rightful place in the Kingdom, but until you go through the process of deliverance, you will not get to your destiny. Don't try to avoid the process of deliverance. Deliverance is a process that we all must go through often. Chains fall, mindsets shift, and identities are restored. You begin to walk differently, think differently, and love differently. The cycle ends because the power behind it has been stripped. Deliverance is Heaven's declaration that your past no longer gets to dictate your future. Decree that over your life: "My past no longer gets to dictate my future!"

This is why Jesus came—to set the captives free, for Luke 4:18 tells us, "*The Spirit of the Lord is upon me, because he hath anointed me to preach the gospel to the poor; he hath sent me to heal the brokenhearted, to preach deliverance to the captives, and recovering of sight to the blind, to set at liberty them that are bruised.*" Deliverance isn't optional for the cycle breaker, it's essential. Because what you're fighting isn't just natural, it's spiritual. And spiritual battles require spiritual weapons. When you experience deliverance, you're not just healed, you're transformed. And what once had the right to follow you no longer has legal access to your life.

Disclaimer:

I would like to take this opportunity to walk through some areas that I believe God has led me to bring to the open space. Some information I will share is not intended to cause disagreements within families but rather to address the issues that we continue to keep closed. Understand the intent is to bring the people of God to full deliverance.

As you proceed with reading this book, The Cycle that Broke, *please keep an open mind and allow God to show you who you are. Allow Him to straighten every crooked place in your life. Read this book, and read it again, until true deliverance becomes a part of your story. Let us begin to open up to receive deliverance. No matter what, this is my story to tell, but it's also God's way to bring forth deliverance.*

Part I

BREAKING THE CYCLES THROUGH DELIVERANCE

Deliverance is the divine process of being set free from bondage—spiritually, emotionally, and mentally. Many people unknowingly live under the weight of cycles that have been passed down through generations, often referred to as *generational curses*. These inherited patterns may include addiction, poverty, abuse, fear, rejection, or destructive behaviors that seem to repeat themselves regardless of efforts to break free. The Bible speaks to these realities in passages like Exodus 20:5, which warns that the sins of the fathers can impact the children to the third and fourth generations. "*Thou shalt not bow down thyself to them, nor serve them: for I the Lord thy God am a jealous God, visiting the iniquity of the fathers upon the children unto the third and fourth generation of them that hate me.*" Deliverance through Christ offers a pathway to identify, confront, and dismantle these long-standing chains. Break the chains and be delivered.

Many struggle to understand why things continue to happen in their life and never get to the root of the problem. We learn the technique of using a bandage, but we never get down to the root of the problem. Staying at the surface and never getting to the root, we ignore many generational cycles that are called *spiritual strongholds,* which are deeply entrenched mindsets, lies, or behaviors that give the enemy access and influence over our lives. These strongholds can blind individuals from the truth of God's Word and keep them trapped in patterns of defeat and discouragement. 2 Corinthians 10:4–5 declares that *"the weapons of our warfare are not carnal but mighty in God for pulling down strongholds."* This means that deliverance is not just about breaking habits but waging spiritual war through prayer, fasting, repentance, and renewing the mind with truth. It is through this intentional spiritual engagement that strongholds are torn down and freedom is restored.

Breaking cycles caused by generational curses and strongholds is not only about personal victory—it's about your legacy and your children's legacy. Deliverance ensures that what once bound a family line ends with you. Repeat that again, but this time make it personal: "What once bound my family line ends with me!" It is a declaration that what held your parents and grandparents will not control your future or the lives of your children. This process is often painful and requires both spiritual discernment and emotional healing, but it leads to restoration, wholeness, and peace. When we choose to confront these hidden forces with the authority of Christ, we open the door for God to rewrite our story and establish a new cycle—one rooted in righteousness, healing, and divine purpose.

Power is released when cycles are broken. Before we get started, let's identify what a cycle represents. A *cycle* is a pattern that repeats, sometimes silently, sometimes loudly, until someone is brave enough to interrupt it. Cycles can be generational, emotional, spiritual, or behavioral. They show up in how we think, how we love, how we parent, how we handle conflict, and even how we pray. Some cycles can be healthy, like the cycle of growth, wisdom, and blessing. But others are toxic like cycles of poverty, abuse, addiction, rejection, fear, unforgiveness, or silence. Ask yourself, "What type of cycle am I dealing with?"

Some of us are living in cycles we didn't choose but we inherited. We don't always recognize them because they're familiar. But just because it's familiar doesn't mean it's right. And just because it's been repeated doesn't mean it must be permanent. We have the power of God living within us that can break any generational curse or stronghold. Tell yourself, "It doesn't matter if my mother did it, or my father did it, it stops with me because my deliverance matters. Breaking these unwanted cycles matters."

WHY BREAKING CYCLES MATTERS

Breaking the cycle is not just about personal healing—it's about creating a lasting legacy. It's about what we pass on and what we put a stop to. When you break a cycle, you are not just freeing yourself; you're unlocking freedom for your children, your children's children, and even your bloodline. Breaking the cycle shifts your family's understanding and direction; it will rewrite your family's identity in Christ and change the trajectory of future generations. When we allow God to partner with us in the breaking, the process becomes sacred. Deliverance comes. Healing flows. And heaven rejoices because what once bound your bloodline is now under your feet.

It matters because cycles have voices—they echo through generations, shaping how families love, speak, cope, believe, and behave. If they are not interrupted, they become inherited prisons. But when you break them, you become a gatekeeper of freedom and a builder of altars for many. Your yes to healing becomes a no to every lie that ran in your family line. It tells fear, addiction, poverty, abuse, and rejection, "This stops here." You begin to plant new seeds of righteousness, faith, truth, and wholeness that will bear fruit long after you're gone.

Breaking the cycle is generational warfare with eternal impact. Eternal impact refers to the lasting spiritual consequences or influence of your actions. The effects that go beyond this life and into eternity. It means what you do now doesn't just change your current circumstances or benefit people in the moment—it echoes in heaven, influences future generations, and aligns with God's eternal purposes. It is one of the most courageous, God-honoring things you can do, not just for yourself but for everyone connected to your name. I decree and declare that every step I take towards breaking my cycle is the beginning of a new journey for my children, family, friends, colleagues, and my enemies—this is true deliverance!

Personal Testimony

The Cycle I Didn't Realize I Had!

I didn't realize I was in a cycle until I started asking, "Why does this keep happening to me?" Why did I keep attracting the same pain in different people? Why did I shut down instead of speaking up? Why did shame feel more natural than joy? I had so many unanswered "whys."

The truth is I was raised in survival, not in safety, meaning that I was taught to be silent and not to tell the truth. I was raised in a home that said, "What's done in this house stays in this house," and that's not a new thing because this is how most people were raised. When you are taught to see it but don't say it, you continue to stay in that vein when you are no longer a child. I experienced abuse as a young mother. I thought that to be beaten meant that I was loved. Think about it; why would he beat me if he didn't love me? Why would he beat me when I was too afraid to do anything to warrant the beating?

I remember that night when I arrived home, I guess it was too late. My daughter was less than a year old. I was about to sit her up in the chair, but the "something" said, "Lay her down in the chair."

I did that and I went and sat on the long chair on the opposite side because I was afraid of the gun that was being held in front of me. Well, when I sat down, the man raised the gun and it went off right over the top of my daughter's head. God was working on my behalf even when I didn't understand; if my daughter had been sitting up in the chair or if I were in the chair holding her, my story would have ended. Lord, I thank you for blocking it. Even as I tell this testimony, I feel tears running down my face. Let me tell you. I watched men abuse a lot of women in my family, so my going through it was no big deal. That generational curse had to break with me.

The woman I became was shaped by wounds no one ever asked me about. Everybody assumed that I am the way that I am because of others; let me tell you, I had to go through something. But God… God stepped in. He didn't just save me. He showed me what I was carrying wasn't mine to keep. I began to confront the trauma that I had experienced, name the patterns of life that continued to follow me, and declare in prayer, "*This cycle ends with me. My children will not experience abuse at the hands of a man—my family will not be abused.*" The cycle stopped with me.

The Bible declares that "No weapon that is formed against thee shall prosper; and every tongue that shall rise against thee in judgment thou shalt condemn." He didn't say that the weapon would not form but it SHALL not prosper. I wrote this book for the one who knows something's not right but can't always put their finger on it. For the one who dares to believe that *just because it runs in your family doesn't mean it has to run through you.* For the one ready to break free. You're not just the one who survived. You're the one who broke the cycle.

Part II

The Personal Cycle

CHAPTER 1

INHERITED PATTERNS

We inherit more than just physical traits—we inherit behaviors, coping mechanisms, and beliefs. These inherited patterns form the emotional blueprint we live by.

These patterns don't always come through harsh words or loud examples; sometimes, they come through what was modeled in silence. We learned how to handle emotions by watching how our parents or the people we love and look up to handle theirs. We picked up on fear even when being told not to be afraid by witnessing how anxiety dominated the atmosphere of our homes or surroundings. The beliefs we hold about ourselves, God, and the world around us were shaped long before we knew how to challenge them. Here is what we must realize: what we inherit doesn't define us. But if we don't confront it, it will continue to lead us.

Inherited patterns are often camouflaged as personality traits or cultural norms. We might say things like, "I've always been like this," or, "That's just how our family is," without realizing that what we've normalized might actually be a form of dysfunction in disguise. This includes generational mindsets about money, relationships, gender roles, and mental health. If no one ever challenged the unhealthy beliefs then those beliefs continue to lead our lives without permission. Negativity will continue to be your foundation because, for you, "I don't want to get above myself," becomes your new language to avoid rejection.

When you confront your pain, you disrupt its power. Avoidance may give you short-term relief, but it gives long-term control to the very patterns that keep you bound. The patterns you inherited will be what control you, no matter how much you believe that you are free. Naming what hurt you, where it came from, and how it shaped you is the first step to dismantling its hold. The truth is what remains hidden often holds the most power. Make a decision today to uncover every area of your life that you have swept under the rug to avoid seeing the truth. When pain is exposed to light, not just any light but God's light, those inherited patterns begin to lose their grip. Healing doesn't happen by accident; it happens by intention. And that intention starts with facing what you once buried. You have to be intentional about your deliverance.

Instability is one of the most common but overlooked inherited patterns. It can come in the form of frequent moves, inconsistent discipline, emotional rollercoaster behavior, or a constant feeling of walking on eggshells. When you grow up without structure or emotional consistency, your nervous system adapts to chaos. It learns to anticipate the worst, scan for danger, and never fully rest. Even as an adult, you may subconsciously seek out unstable relationships or intentionally interfere with your own peace because it feels unfamiliar. Breaking the cycle of instability means learning how to sit with calm, trust steady love, and embrace the safety God provides. God is the only one who can deliver you from the chaos bondage. Once you are free, you will wake up in the morning with words of affirmation that say, "Today is going to be a great day," or, "I am free from chaos and instability." You will find yourself smiling and have no explanation for why you are smiling. All you will know is that you have broken free from the mess that had you unstable.

Emotional Wounds, Fear, and Shame

Some of us were born into households where emotional wounds were the norm. Our parents, uncles, and aunts were broken themselves—doing the best they could with what they had but often passing down the very pain they never healed from. We learned early on that expressing emotions was unsafe, that vulnerability was a weakness, and that being "strong" meant being silent. I remember that, as a child, my cousin was asked to babysit my sibling and me. Nothing out of the norm, except this particular day, she asked us to fill up the bathtub. Thinking that I was doing a great job, I filled it to the top, not realizing that I would get my first opportunity to see how long I could hold my breath underwater. My cousin took my head and held it underwater. How did I survive? Only by the grace of God. I learned early on that if we are not careful, we will take the anger that we feel and abuse another person if we are not delivered. To this day—well, maybe not anymore, I never shared this. I was afraid I would hold it against my cousin because I know now that it was a spirit that controlled her. Remember that we do not wrestle with flesh and blood—it's those evil spirits that try to control the mind and body.

Fear became a companion—fear of rejection, of abandonment, of not being enough. And when fear wasn't present, shame took its place. Shame that whispered, *"You're too much."* *"You're not enough."* *"You're the problem."* Shame that made us shrink, apologize for existing, or overcompensate by trying to be perfect. These emotions, when left unhealed, build spiritual and emotional cages. We live inside them, call them "normal," and even teach them to our children without realizing we are shaping their view of love, worth, and identity.

Emotional wounds, especially those sustained in childhood, leave invisible scars that influence how we see ourselves and how we navigate the world. We may fear abandonment because someone left us or struggle with intimacy because love was used as leverage. These wounds shape how we respond to correction, receive affection, and trust others. The fear becomes a filter and shame becomes a false identity. But what was once your survival mechanism doesn't have to be your life sentence. God wants to heal what you didn't cause—and restore what you didn't even know was broken.

Left untreated, these wounds fester and become a lens through which we interpret every experience. We begin to anticipate rejection, sabotage intimacy, and distrust genuine love—not because people are necessarily unsafe but because the pain in us has not yet found closure. Emotional wounds that remain unhealed eventually shape how we treat ourselves. We punish ourselves for not being enough and we shrink back from purpose out of fear of being exposed. But the love of God reaches into the hidden corners of our hearts and rewrites the narratives that shame tried to write in permanent ink.

Silence, Self-Doubt, and People-Pleasing

You may not remember the first time you decided to stay quiet instead of speaking up, but your body does. Silence was a form of safety. You stayed silent to avoid conflict, to avoid punishment, to keep peace in a home where peace was rarely present. Over time, that silence became your default—even when you were old enough to speak and strong enough to be heard. I am still learning to speak up; sometimes, staying quiet is the best approach to avoid confusion and confrontation. Today, I will ask the Lord to remove the muzzle.

Self-doubt became your language. You questioned your worth, second-guessed your decisions, and looked to others for validation because trusting yourself felt like a foreign concept. You were taught, not in words but in responses, that your voice didn't matter, that your presence was too much, or that your needs came last. And so you became a *people pleaser*. People-pleasing is one of the most deceptive inherited behaviors because it often looks like kindness on the surface—but underneath, it's rooted in fear. When you've been conditioned to associate love with approval, you learn to perform for affection. You begin to silence your needs to meet everyone else's. You say yes when you want to say no. You shape-shift to avoid conflict or rejection. Over time, you lose your sense of self because pleasing others becomes your identity. But God did not call you to be a puppet of people's expectations. He called you to walk in truth, even when it's uncomfortable. Freedom begins when you stop living to be accepted—and start living from the acceptance you already have in Christ.

You learned how to read the room, how to adapt, how to smile even when it hurts. You were praised for being "so helpful" and "so easygoing," but deep inside, you were unraveling—because being liked came at the cost of being known. I was connecting with the wrong people so that I could hide behind them just to feel a little happiness. Somehow, I knew I deserved better, but where was the strength going to come from to speak?

Breaking this pattern begins with awareness, recognizing that some of the 'strength' you carry is actually unprocessed pain. That some of the ways you show up in relationships are rooted in trauma, not truth. That silence is not strength when it stifles your healing. You can honor your past while refusing to repeat it. You can love your family and still confront the patterns. You can acknowledge the survival skills you've learned while deciding that you are ready to live, not just survive. Because cycles don't break with blame—they break with boldness.

Prayer to Break Inherited Patterns

Father God, I come before You in humility, recognizing that some of the struggles I face did not begin with me. Lord, I acknowledge the generational patterns—spoken and unspoken, seen and unseen— that have been passed down through my family line. Cycles of fear, rejection, abandonment, addiction, poverty, anger, and silence have followed us for far too long.

But today, I draw the bloodline of Jesus Christ between me and everything that has tried to follow me from generations past. Your Word says in Galatians 3:13 that "*Christ has redeemed us from the curse of the law*." So, I declare that I am redeemed. The old patterns are broken by the power of Jesus' sacrifice.

I renounce every inherited mindset and behavior that does not align with Your will for my life. I reject fear and choose faith. I release shame and receive Your grace. I cancel self-doubt and declare Your truth over my identity.

God, heal the wounds that I didn't cause but still carry. Heal my heart, renew my mind, and purify my spirit. Where there was generational bondage let there now be generational blessings. Where there was silence let there be the sound of praise. Where there was confusion let clarity come. Where there was pain let peace reign.

Holy Spirit, guide me in new patterns. Teach me how to speak life, to walk in freedom, and to model righteousness for the generations after me. Let the cycle break with me and let Your legacy of love and truth begin now.

In Jesus' mighty name, Amen.

CHAPTER 2

TRAUMA ON REPEAT

Trauma doesn't always scream. Sometimes, it whispers through your habits, relationships, and inner dialogue. It becomes embedded in your nervous system, repeating itself in ways you don't always recognize—until you do. Some of us were raised in environments where abuse—verbal, emotional, physical, or even spiritual—was normalized. Maybe it came from a parent, a spouse, a significant other, or a place where you should have felt safe. Instead of being nurtured, you were neglected, criticized, controlled, or silenced. That trauma didn't end with the person who hurt you. It began a cycle of re-creation: reliving similar pain in different places, with different faces. We have learned to ignore trauma because of what we believe trauma looks like. If it's not bleeding, it's not trauma. This is far from the truth. Bleeding is not always visible—some bleeding occurs inside.

Internal trauma will make you reject the help you need because you can't see it. Or you may have learned to become hyper-independent because asking for help was met with rejection. You may have mastered emotional detachment because connection felt dangerous.

These patterns form silently but powerfully—teaching you how to protect yourself at the cost of authentic living. The problem is *what protected you in one season can imprison you in the next.* God's desire isn't just to keep you safe—it's to make you whole. Lord, I want to be made whole.

Abuse, what does it look like? It often disguises itself as control or discipline. It teaches you that love must hurt, that acceptance comes at the cost of your voice, and that silence is safer than truth. When abuse is normalized, it gets passed on in tone, in temper, in the unspoken rules that govern a household. And unless it's confronted, it multiplies. Abuse is passed down. We find ourselves in relationships that mimic our past. We live in the same fear that we have seen others have. We sabotage our peace. However, deliverance and healing interrupt that pattern. Awareness is the first step. Accepting deliverance is a form of therapy and knowing the truth brings freedom. The Bible says, in James 8:32, *"And ye shall know the truth, and the truth shall make you free."* Without freedom, you accept poverty because it teaches you to expect lack. Instability becomes the norm and living a stable life becomes abnormal.

Poverty is also a kind of trauma. It's not just about a lack of money—it's about a lack of access, stability, opportunity, and sometimes dignity. Growing up in "survival mode" teaches you that needs will always go unmet, that there's never enough, and that dreams are luxuries you can't afford. That mindset can follow you into adulthood, even if your income changes your belief in scarcity doesn't. I didn't realize that until I was delivered from a poverty mindset. I would even put word curses on myself by saying things like, "I'm broke," or, "I can't afford that." No matter what it was. Just know, poverty is more than a lack of money—it is a mindset of scarcity that can infiltrate every area of life. It tells you there's never enough—of resources, of support, or opportunity. It teaches you to operate from fear, to hoard instead of give, to survive instead of dream. Even when your bank account changes, the poverty mindset can linger if it's never healed. Jesus, help your people. Even when you get the promotion that you prayed for, you still say, "I can afford that!" We need to be delivered from the yoke of bondage called poverty.

Instability becomes your norm—whether emotional, financial, or relational. You expect the worst because you've seen it too many times. You don't trust good things because they've always come with strings. And so, unconsciously, you sabotage peace because chaos feels more familiar. Instability teaches you that chaos is normal. When you've lived with constant unpredictability—where emotions fluctuate, love is conditional, or homes and jobs come and go—you begin to distrust consistency. You brace for the next breakdown because peace feels foreign. This instability becomes internalized, making it difficult to feel safe even in safe places. It's an uncomfortable feeling when I hear someone say, "I expect the worst but pray for the best!" I never understand why we pray for the best yet don't trust God to give us what we pray for. But because we deal with instability, it leads us to expect the worst. Ask yourself, why are you praying?

How Unhealed Wounds Repeat Themselves

Trauma unhealed is trauma repeated—it may not look the same, but it *feels* the same. You find yourself in relationships that mirror the dysfunction you grew up in. You recreate toxic patterns, not because you want to but because your soul is trying to resolve a wound that was never treated. You over-function in spaces where you're undervalued. You love with walls up. You isolate yourself when things get hard. And at the root of it all is not weakness—but woundedness. My whole life in one paragraph. The enemy uses trauma to keep you stuck. But God uses awareness to pull you out. Healing doesn't erase the past, but it interrupts the pattern. It says, "What happened to me was real, but it won't define me." It begins with acknowledgment, moves through honesty, and is completed through God's grace, forgiveness, and time. It's time for us to be healed entirely by removing the bandage, allowing us to feel the air, so that we can heal properly.

When you confront your pain, you disrupt its power.

Jeremiah 30:17 says, *"But I will restore you to health and heal your wounds,' declares the Lord."*

A direct promise of restoration and healing for all forms of deep emotional and spiritual pain.

Prayer: Breaking the Cycle of Repeated Trauma

Father God, I come to You today weary from the weight of repeated pain. Lord, I've seen the same hurt resurface in different seasons, different faces, and different situations. It feels like a cycle I can't escape—abuse, abandonment, instability, rejection. I carry wounds that never seem to fully heal and I confess, God, that I am tired.

But I also know that You are the Healer of all wounds and the Breaker of all chains. You said in Psalm 147:3 that You heal the brokenhearted and bind up their wounds. So today, I give You my brokenness. I give You the patterns I don't fully understand. I give You the parts of me that still flinch from the past, even when the moment has long passed.

God, I ask You to go deep into the hidden places of my soul—the trauma buried beneath the surface, the pain I've tried to numb, the memories I've tried to forget. Shine Your light in the darkness and uproot what has taken hold of me.

I break agreement with every lie that trauma has taught me—lies that I'm unworthy, unloved, or unseen. I declare Your truth over my life: I am chosen, I am whole, and I am Yours.

Jesus, help me to recognize the signs of repeated trauma before they take root again. Give me discernment, strength, and courage to walk away from what harms me and run toward what heals me. Replace instability with peace, confusion with clarity, fear with boldness.

Let the trauma end with me. Let my healing begin today. And let my life become a testimony that You can redeem even the most broken stories.

In the name of Jesus—the One who restores all things— Amen.

Chapter 3

<THE BREAKING POINT>

THE BREAKING POINT

Every cycle has a center. A point where pain, patterns, and pressure collide. And for many of us, it's not a gentle moment—it's a breaking point.

The breaking point often doesn't look spiritual at first. It looks like exhaustion. Like weeping in silence. Like saying, "I can't live like this anymore." It's the moment you realize something in your life must shift—or else you will be stuck in a loop that costs you your peace, your joy, and even your purpose. This is why healing is significant because it helps us to find ways to deal with our inner self before we reach the point of no return.

For me, the breaking point came in a season where I was tired of pretending. Tired of carrying everyone else's expectations. Tired of fighting battles that weren't mine and bleeding from wounds I didn't cause. I was still functioning—but I was fractured. Smiling, but silently suffocating. Dealing with abuse, being called out of my name for no reason at all. Hating the person that I was. I hated anyone looking at me. In my mind, they could see every open wound. It felt like they could literally see the blood leaking from my wounds that I thought I had covered. I was at my breaking point. I didn't think there was anything else I could do, anywhere else that I could go, or if anyone else was out there to help me heal.

That's when I cried out—not a rehearsed, polished prayer but a broken whisper: "God, help me. I can't do this anymore."

When Enough Is Enough

There is sacredness in reaching your limit. It's not a sign of failure. It's often the doorway to freedom. Because when you reach the end of yourself, you make room for the beginning of God's intervention. This is the point at which you let go and allow God to work in you.

Some people break cycles quietly—through a decision, a prayer, or a boundary. Others break it dramatically—through a divorce, a move, a breakdown, or a confrontation. Either way, the moment is holy. It's the place where transformation begins.

The breaking point is, in fact, the *turning* point.

It's when you stop asking, "Why me?" and start asking, "What now?"

It's when you stop waiting for someone else to fix it and start partnering with God to change it.

It's when you get honest—with yourself, with your pain, with your patterns—and finally say: "This cannot continue."

The Break Isn't the End—It's the Beginning

We often fear breaking. But in God's hands, breaking leads to building. Building leads to having and having leads to a great relationship with God.

Like Mary of Bethany, the woman with the alabaster box in Luke 7, your breaking becomes an offering. Like Jacob wrestling with the angel in Genesis 32, your breaking leads to a name change, a destiny shift. Like Jesus at the Last Supper, the breaking precedes multiplication. You are not falling apart. You are falling into alignment. Don't fear the breaking point. Welcome it. Because it's there that the cycle begins to tremble, the curse begins to crack. The silence is shattered. And you that God designed—healed, whole, and free—starts to rise.

Can you imagine your unhealed self meeting up with your healed self? There would be no match. The unhealed you had to break in order for the BEGINNING new you to come forth. Think about that woman in Luke 7, who is considered a "sinner", who washes Jesus' feet with her hair and anoints His feet. She had to be at her breaking point to know that she was a sinner, but she just had to get close to Him by any means necessary. Jesus gave her a new beginning by forgiving her sins. Your breaking point isn't the end—it's truly the beginning.

Prayer: At the Breaking Point

Father God, I come before You with a heart that feels stretched beyond its limits. I am at the breaking point—physically tired, emotionally drained, and spiritually worn. I don't have the answers. I don't have the strength. But I still have You.

Lord, You said in Psalm 34:18 that You are near to the brokenhearted and save those who are crushed in spirit. I need You to be near right now. I'm standing at the edge of what I can handle and I'm asking You to step in and carry what I cannot.

I confess that I've tried to fix it on my own. I've cried in silence. I've smiled to hide the pain. I've pushed through, hoping it would get better. But now I lay it all down. Every burden. Every tear. Every shattered piece.

God, let this breaking point be my turning point.

Break the cycles that keep repeating. Break the patterns that keep sabotaging my peace. Break the silence where truth needs to speak. And in place of the brokenness, build something unshakable—my faith, my identity, my purpose.

I believe You are not just the God of comfort but the God of breakthroughs. So right here, at my lowest, I invite You to do what only You can do. Restore me. Redirect me. Revive me.

Let this be the moment everything shifts.

In Jesus' name, Amen.

CHAPTER 4

<WHAT RUNS IN THE FAMILY>

WHAT RUNS IN THE FAMILY

There's a saying: *"It runs in the family."* Usually, it's said in reference to traits—like creativity, athletic ability, the way you walk, talk, or even a laugh. But what happens when what "runs in the family" is trauma, brokenness, or spiritual bondage? Something to think about. We brag about doing things just like our family, but what we miss is the acts of bondage that we are replaying in our lives daily.

Just think about this; there are some things that your family does that you dislike. It could be a parent, siblings, cousins, an auntie, or an uncle, but they do things that you do not like. Believe it or not, you carry that same trait. The very thing that you do not want in them YOU ARE THEM! It is because generational cycles don't start with you, but they can end with you.

What is a generational curse? A generational curse refers to the transmission of negative patterns, behaviors, or consequences from one generation to the next, often rooted in spiritual, emotional, or behavioral issues that were never addressed or healed. These can manifest as cycles of addiction, abuse, poverty, broken relationships, or spiritual bondage. Rather than being a random event or situation that brings hardship or suffering, generational curses are often deeply ingrained in family histories, passed down through learned behaviors, traumatic experiences, or spiritual strongholds. Breaking these cycles requires intentional reflection, spiritual intervention, and a commitment to healing—both for oneself and future generations.

When Patterns Become Inheritance

Some families pass down wealth. Others pass down wounds. What begins as one person's trauma becomes the next generation's normal. Abuse is passed down as discipline. Manipulation is masked as love. Silence is mistaken for strength. And what should have been corrected becomes protected. We inherit more than genetics—we inherit belief systems and emotional patterns. What one generation excuses the next generation repeats. But the good news? You don't have to inherit what God never intended you to carry. It's time for you to release the baggage and bondage.

Breaking the Lineage of Bondage

Scripture acknowledges the impact of generational sin. *"I, the Lord your God, am a jealous God, punishing the children for the sin of the parents to the third and fourth generation…"*
—Exodus 20:5

But that's not where the story ends. *"…but showing love to a thousand generations of those who love me and keep my commandments."*
—Exodus 20:6

This tells us two things:

1. Yes, generational sin and strongholds are real.
2. But God's mercy is greater than any curse.

When you stand up and say, "It stops here," you are not just protecting your future—you are reaching back to heal your past. You are becoming a repairer of the breach (Isaiah 58:12), a cycle breaker, a generational curse crusher. You are the answered prayer of someone who didn't survive long enough to see the cycle end. You have to know that God chose you to be the cycle breaker in your family. Not only does your life depend on it, but your family's life depends on it as well.

When you stand up and say, "It stops here," you are declaring that the pain, trauma, and dysfunction that ran through generations will not continue through you. This bold stance invites God's restoration to flow through your bloodline, redeeming what was broken and rewriting what was spoken. Your decision to break the cycle becomes a divine interruption—one that blesses not only your children but your parents and even those who came before. What once seemed like a burden becomes a bridge to breakthrough. This is the power of healing from the inside out.

Prayer: Breaking What Runs in the Family

Father God, Today, I stand in the gap for my bloodline. I acknowledge the things that have run in my family—patterns of dysfunction, addiction, broken relationships, mental torment, poverty, abuse, rejection, and spiritual oppression. But I also declare this truth: What has run in my family ends with me.

Your Word says in Ezekiel 18:20 that the child will not be punished for the parent's sins. So I come out of agreement with every generational curse, every soul tie, every inherited mindset that contradicts Your truth.

In the name of Jesus, I break every cycle that has passed down through generations. I break off inherited fear, bitterness, control, pride, and shame. I break off silence, suppression, and secrecy. I break off every word curse spoken over my family line. I cancel the assignment of the enemy that has tried to hijack my family's destiny.

I declare that from this point forward, blessings will flow instead of bondage. Healing will replace hurt. Joy will replace sorrow. Generational trauma will give way to generational testimonies. What was tolerated in the past will no longer be accepted. A new standard is rising and I choose to walk in it.

God, use me as a disruptor. Let my obedience become the turning point. Let my surrender become the starting point of a new legacy—one rooted in Your Word, Your power, and Your love.

I thank You that by the blood of Jesus, I am covered, redeemed, and set apart. This is where the cycle breaks. This is where the healing begins. This is where freedom flows.

In Jesus' powerful name, Amen.

CHAPTER 5

THE SILENT INHERITANCE

Not everything that was passed down is spoken. Some inheritances are silent—woven into the atmosphere of our childhood homes, tucked between the pauses in conversations, and etched into the way love, anger, or distance was expressed. You don't always realize you've inherited something until you start living your adult life and wonder, *Why am I like this?* I need to encourage you to get delivered; for deliverance is the only way to recognize or even acknowledge the need for change.

Many families never talk about their pain. What happened is either denied, downplayed, or drowned in distraction. The trauma is buried, but the fruit of it shows up in generations that follow— through anxiety, control issues, fear of vulnerability, or distrust of love. We learn more from *what wasn't said* than we realize.

Silence Teaches Too

If no one talked about feelings, you learned to suppress yours. If no one apologized, you learned to carry blame that wasn't yours. If no one modeled safety, you confused love with chaos.

This kind of silence is heavy. It teaches us to carry pain in secret, to perform instead of process, and to smile when our souls are breaking. But the silence you inherited does not have to be the silence you pass down. I remember going through many rough seasons in my life that I refused to share because I didn't want anyone to downplay what I was going through. It happened because I had a conversation with my best friend when I was in my 20s. I was being beaten and threatened every day and I was afraid to leave because I was told that if I left, he would kill me. Living in fear, I shared it only with my best friend. Her response was, "If you want to leave, you will leave; you just want to stay in the abuse!"

That hurt me because of my fear of leaving. I had two kids and didn't want to die trying to save their lives. So I stayed and continued to suffer in silence. In my mind, if I shared what I was going through, no one would care, so I didn't share. I wanted healing to begin, so I started praying as best as I could. One of the things I had to do was find the courage to speak out. So, when we gain the courage to name what was never named, God can heal what has never been healed.

What your mother couldn't talk about you can confront. What your father never healed from you can grieve and release. What your family feared you can face—with wisdom, with God, and with support from the right people. When you speak truth into silence, you don't dishonor your family—you redeem it. You become the one who no longer carries the wound forward but chooses to build something new. You are the one who dares to break the silence—and with it, you are breaking the cycle.

Prayer: Breaking the Silent Inheritance

Father God, I come before You today carrying things I never chose—things passed down not through words but through silence. I inherited the silence that came from generations who didn't know how to talk about pain, grief, fear, or love. I inherited suppressed emotions, unspoken trauma, and unhealed wounds.

Lord, I lift up the pain that was never named. The tears that were never validated. The questions that were never answered. I confess that silence has shaped how I see myself, how I relate to others, and how I experience You. But I don't want to live bound by what was never spoken.

You are the God who speaks—who creates with Your voice, who heals with Your Word, who breaks chains with truth. So today, I ask You to speak into every silent place in my soul. Shine Your light into what was hidden. Bring language to what was buried. Bring healing to what was passed down in whispers and shadows.

I break agreement with the belief that silence is strength. I declare that honesty is holy and vulnerability is not weakness. I release the pressure to carry what others never had the tools to face. I choose truth. I choose healing. I choose to start the conversation that was never had.

Let me be the one who says what was never said. Who feels what was never allowed. Who prays what was never taught. Who loves without fear. Let the inheritance I leave behind be one of wholeness, truth, and freedom.

In Jesus' name, Amen.

CHAPTER 6

BECOMING THE DISRUPTOR

B reaking a cycle doesn't start with healing—it starts with disruption. A disruptor is someone who interrupts what is familiar, expected, or generational, especially when that 'normal' is unhealthy, toxic, or ungodly. To disrupt something means to interrupt its usual course. It means being the one who "no longer follows the script," even when the script is familiar, expected, or generationally reinforced. Disruptors don't wait for permission—they move in obedience, even when it's uncomfortable.

But let me share that becoming a disruptor is not glamorous. It costs something. However, what it produces is freedom. Disruptors are often misunderstood because they break patterns people have grown comfortable with—even if those patterns are harmful. Spiritually, disruptors are often called and anointed by God to confront strongholds and stand in the gap for their bloodline. I frequently wondered how God could use me to start a family prayer call for my family when I wasn't the preacher, pastor, or minister of the family. One thing to remember is that when you have been called and anointed by God, He does not follow man's schedule or man's calendar. He will do just what He says. I am called by God to be the disruptor in my family. I am often faced with opposition, but I never stop praying for my family. Do you know your position? Do you know that you have been called to stand out, not to fit in?

What Does It Cost to Break the Cycle?

To break cycles, you will likely be the one who is misunderstood. If you can't handle being talked about or being lied to, you have to go to God and ask Him to give you the strength needed to make it. Don't pray that He removes the pressure, but ask Him to make you strong in the Holy Ghost. To break cycles, you will be the one who chooses therapy when others prefer silence. The one who says, "That's not okay," when everyone else shrugs. The one who prays boldly, sets boundaries, walks away from dysfunction, and refuses to apologize for growing away from mess. Decree and declare over your life that you "refuse to apologize for growing in God!"

It may mean distancing yourself from what's familiar. It may mean confronting family members who don't want to deal with the truth. It may mean losing relationships that were rooted in shared brokenness. However, understand this: healing will always offend those who are *committed to staying wounded.* You are not betraying your family—you are freeing your bloodline. You're not trying to be better than anyone; you're trying to become who God created you to be. You need to be healed by your family before you can fight the demons on behalf of your family.

Obedience over Comfort

God often calls the disruptor from within. You don't need a platform to break cycles. You need obedience, discernment, and a willingness to walk with God even when no one else understands. *"I have set you apart from the nations…"* —Leviticus 20:26. *"Come out from among them and be separate…"* —2 Corinthians 6:17. You were chosen to stand out—for a holy reason. To speak up. To say no. To draw a line in the sand. To call things what they are so that God can heal them.

You may be the first to confront dysfunction. But because of you, you won't be the last to walk in wholeness. *You Are the Disruptor. The Deliverer. The One Who Stands in the Gap.* When you step into this role, you are not just disrupting trauma—you are partnering with heaven. You are reversing generational curses and ushering in generational blessings. It's not always easy, but it's always worth it. And heaven is backing you.

Prayer: Becoming the Disruptor

Father God, You have called me to be different—for a divine reason. Not to fit in but to stand out. Not to conform but to transform. I may not have asked for this assignment, but I embrace it now: I am the one You have chosen to disrupt the cycle.

Give me the strength to stand where others have fallen. Give me the courage to speak when others have stayed silent. Make me bold enough to draw the line, even when it's lonely. I declare that with Your power, I am breaking the patterns that plagued my bloodline—cycles of trauma, dysfunction, addiction, spiritual apathy, and emotional bondage.

I know being a disruptor comes with resistance—but I also know that obedience brings breakthrough. So I choose obedience. I choose holiness over history. I choose legacy over comfort. I choose to follow Your voice even when it contradicts the noise of tradition.

Anoint me to walk in authority—not in my own strength but by Your Spirit. Let me carry truth with compassion, conviction with humility, and fire with grace. May my life echo in generations to come—not because I was perfect but because I was willing.

I may be the first in my family to say, "Enough." The first to seek help. The first to pray out loud. The first to walk in freedom. But I won't be the last.

Let my obedience start a ripple that becomes a revolution. Let the cycles end and a new era begin—with You at the center.

In the mighty, chain-breaking name of Jesus, Amen.

Part III
The Spiritual Cycle

CHAPTER 7

STRONGHOLDS IN THE SPIRIT

Not all cycles are emotional or behavioral—some are spiritual. There are patterns that logic can't explain, therapy can't diagnose, and willpower can't fix. Although there is nothing wrong with therapy, don't look for therapy to be the only answer to what you're going through. The pattern of behavior is not just a habit or a generational tendency—they are strongholds and they must be broken in the spirit before they can be healed in the natural. Please allow that to sink in. You only want to look good on the outside because that's what man sees but ignore the destruction on the inside that you need to get rid of. Those destructive behaviors cannot be dealt with on the surface; you must go into the spiritual realm to destroy those demonic forces.

"For the weapons of our warfare are not carnal but mighty through God to the pulling down of strongholds."—2 Corinthians 10:4

A stronghold is a fortified lie. It's a deeply rooted belief or demonic force that keeps you bound to fear, shame, addiction, confusion, or rebellion. These strongholds form over time—through trauma, through agreement with lies, and spiritual inheritance. They are reinforced by life experiences and protected by silence.

Identifying the Strongholds

Some strongholds hide in plain sight. You think it's just how you are—but it's not you, it's what attached itself to you:

- A constant fear of abandonment that shows up in every relationship
- An inability to trust—even when people are good to you
- Cycles of addiction—to substances, people, or even approval
- A pattern of self-sabotage the moment things start to go well
- Bitterness that refuses to let go, no matter how many times you forgive
- A deep-rooted rejection that interprets every "no" as a personal attack
- Lust, anger, confusion, or spiritual apathy that keeps you stuck

These are not just personality quirks. They are spiritual imprisonment. And freedom doesn't come from trying harder—it comes from going deeper.

The Battle Is Spiritual

When you are dealing with a stronghold, the only way to win is to fight with spiritual weapons: the Word of God, prayer, fasting, worship, and repentance. You must renounce what you unknowingly agreed with. You must speak truth where lies have ruled. And you must call on the power and authority of Jesus Christ, the only One strong enough to tear down what's been built up over generations.

"If the Son sets you free, you will be free indeed." - John 8:36

Strongholds are persistent—but they are not permanent. They tremble at the name of Jesus. They break under the anointing. They collapse when truth is spoken with faith. So, ask yourself, "Why am I holding on to a stronghold that can be broken at the Name of Jesus?" When you begin to tell GOD that you refuse to be bound and ask Him to break every stronghold in your life I know He will do it because He did it for me. Strongholds were broken. If you don't like me, I'm okay with that. If you talk about me, I'm okay with that. I will NEVER be bound again with the yoke of bondage.

"Stand fast therefore in the liberty wherewith Christ hath made us free and be not entangled again with the yoke of bondage." – Galatian 5:1

Freedom Is Your Birthright

You were never meant to live in bondage. Freedom is not for the few—it's the inheritance of every child of God. When you begin to address the spiritual roots of your cycles, healing accelerates. The fog of bondage lifts. The weight begins to decrease. And the ground beneath your feet starts to shift, for the good. Don't be afraid of the strongholds—become aware of your authority. Don't try to hide them because of fear; face them head-on and be delivered. You don't have to live another day entangled in what Jesus already defeated. The cycle breaks when you bind what's been binding you and loose the Word of God over your life. You are not just fighting for yourself. You're breaking spiritual chains for those who come after you.

Enjoy your birthright and live out what Jesus did on the cross for your salvation.

Prayer: Breaking Strongholds in the Spirit

Father God, In the name of Jesus, I come before You recognizing that not all battles are physical—some are deeply spiritual. Lord, I acknowledge the strongholds that have taken root in my heart, my mind, and my spirit. These strongholds—of fear, rejection, pride, addiction, insecurity, shame, bitterness, control, and unbelief—are lies that have tried to build fortresses where Your truth should reign.

But today, I rise up in spiritual authority and declare: these strongholds must fall.

Your Word says in 2 Corinthians 10:4–5 that the weapons of our warfare are not carnal but mighty through You for the pulling down of strongholds. So I take up the weapons You've given me—prayer, fasting, Your Word, and the blood of Jesus—and I come against every high thing that exalts itself against the knowledge of You.

I tear down the walls of deception. I cast out every spirit of confusion. I bind the lies of the enemy and loose the truth of God in my life. I command every demonic assignment to be cancelled. Every generational spirit of bondage must go. Every hidden agreement with darkness is broken.

Lord, renew my mind. Let Your truth take root where the enemy once had influence. Replace fear with faith, rejection with acceptance, shame with grace, and bondage with freedom. I declare that I am no longer a prisoner—I am a child of God and whom the Son sets free is free indeed (John 8:36).

I submit every area of my life to You—my thoughts, emotions, desires, and habits. Let them align with Your Spirit. Let Your Holy Fire consume every residue of darkness. And let me walk boldly in the liberty You paid for at Calvary. From this moment on, I live free. The strongholds are shattered. The chains are broken. Victory is mine—through Jesus Christ.

In His mighty name, Amen.

CHAPTER 8

WHEN GOD STEPS IN

Cycles break when human effort meets divine intervention.

There comes a moment in every journey where counseling, journaling, boundaries, and self-reflection aren't enough—because some battles are not just emotional, they're spiritual. Some cycles don't just need clarity; they need to be delivered. I recall trying to use journaling as a means of deliverance, but it didn't work. You often hear people say, "Just write it down and you'll be healed." And while that might help with certain things, it doesn't work when you're bound by something you don't even fully understand. You can't heal what you haven't recognized as warfare. The truth is it's hard to get free when the battle is happening inside of you. As humans, we tend to chase what we desire and cling to what feels good, even when it's harmful. It's easy to analyze someone else's struggle and become the perfect therapist—until you're staring down the same battle yourself and, suddenly, the advice you once gave feels out of reach. And that's why we need God to step in.

The God Who Interrupts Cycles

God has a history of stepping into generational mess and rewriting bloodlines. If you don't believe me, let's look at the Bible. You are guaranteed to see your story. Look at Abraham—called away from a pagan family into a covenant. Look at Joseph—used to redeem a family that rejected him. Look at Rahab—delivered from a cycle of shame and chosen for legacy. Look at YOU—called, chosen, and set apart.

When God steps in, cycles are not just broken—they're reversed. Where there was a curse now there is a blessing. Where there was dysfunction now there is destiny. Where there was silence now there is sound—of freedom, of truth, of healing. Where despair once lingered now hope takes root and multiplies. Where families were fractured restoration begins. The chains that once held generations hostage begin to fall, one by one, as God's power rewrites the story. His presence doesn't just change the outcome—it shifts the entire atmosphere. What was meant for evil becomes the very soil where purpose grows. When God steps in, demons get running. No matter what your battle is, know that you have strength in God.

The Tools God Uses

God steps in through deliverance—but also through your willingness to complete the process.

1. Prayer shatters strongholds and opens your spiritual eyes.
2. Fasting breaks dependency and aligns your spirit with God's.
3. The Word of God reprograms your thinking and heals your heart.
4. The Holy Spirit becomes your internal Guide and Comforter.

5. Community brings accountability, healing, and testimony.

You'll begin to see shifts in your life that you can't explain but can only attribute to God's hand. Doors close that need to. Mindsets that are used to rule you break away. Things you used to tolerate start to feel foreign. That's not a coincidence—that's deliverance. Let me say that again; you have been delivered!

From Surviving to Thriving

When God steps in, He doesn't just stop the bleeding—He starts the building. He rebuilds your confidence. Restores your identity. Renews your joy. He teaches you how to live whole, not just healed. God doesn't just want to break the cycle—He wants to birth something new in its place. He is not only the Chain-Breaker; He is the Legacy-Maker.

You've tried fixing it your way. Now let God finish it His way.

He doesn't just mend what was torn—He creates something entirely new. He takes the ashes of what was and forms beauty. He takes the confusion and gives clarity. He doesn't just restore what was lost—He multiplies what was surrendered. Your story becomes a declaration that His power is greater than your past and that His promises still stand.

Prayer: When God Steps In

Father God, I thank You that You are not a distant God. You are not silent in my pain or absent in my chaos. You are the God who steps in. And when You step in, everything shifts.

You step into broken homes and begin to restore. You step into dark places and speak light.

You step into the middle of cycles, curses, trauma, and confusion— and You rewrite the story.

God, I invite You into every area of my life. Step into the rooms I've closed off out of fear. Step into the memories I've buried. Step into the wounds I've tried to heal on my own. I give You full access. Come and interrupt what has tried to define me.

When You step in, the curse turns into a blessing. Dysfunction turns into destiny. Silence turns into sound—of freedom, healing, and truth. You don't just stop the bleeding; You start the building.

You rebuild what was torn down. You restore what was stolen. You redeem what was wasted. I thank You that You are not just the Chain-Breaker—You are the Legacy-Maker. You don't just remove what's broken; You replace it with something beautiful.

Lord, I release control and make room for Your divine movement. I've tried it my way—but now I trust Your way. Step into my family, my mind, my habits, my finances, my relationships, my ministry. Do what only You can do.

I believe that when You step in, cycles don't just break—they stay broken. New patterns begin. New purpose is born. And legacy is rewritten.

Thank You for stepping in.

In Jesus' mighty name, Amen.

CHAPTER 9

RENEWING THE MIND

Breaking the cycle in your spirit is powerful—but to *sustain* your freedom, you must break the cycle in your mind. Because even after deliverance, your thoughts will try to drag you back to what God already freed you from. Renewing the mind is a transformative process that involves replacing old, negative, or worldly patterns of thinking with God's truth. It is not a one-time event but a daily commitment to align our thoughts with Scripture. As we meditate on God's Word, we begin to see ourselves, others, and our circumstances through His perspective. This renewal leads to spiritual growth, emotional healing, and clearer discernment.

"Do not be conformed to this world, but be transformed by the renewing of your mind..."—Romans 12:2

When our minds are renewed, our lives begin to reflect the will of God—what is good, pleasing, and perfect. This is where true transformation begins. You cannot walk into freedom with a mindset still chained to the past. Your mindset must shift to match your miracle. The old way of thinking—rooted in fear, doubt, and survival—must be replaced with the truth of God's Word. Renewing the mind is not a one-time event but a daily decision to believe what God says over what life has shown you. As your thoughts align with His promises, you will begin to see the cycles that once held you break in plain view and the life He intended for you unfold.

Rewiring What Life Taught You

When you've lived under a cycle of fear, rejection, or lack, your mind becomes wired to expect it—even after you're no longer in that environment. You might be out of the cycle physically but mentally still trapped in a form of rejection that is somewhat hard to recognize.

1. Thinking you'll never be enough.
2. Expecting disappointment before it arrives.
3. Distrusting peace because chaos always followed.
4. Believing your past disqualifies your future.

This is why renewing your mind is not optional, it's essential. You can't build a new life with old thinking. Rejection had disqualified you, not God. Rejection is one of the deepest wounds a person can experience because it attacks your identity at the core. It whispers that you are not wanted or that you do not belong. Rejection can come from family, friends, relationships, or even opportunities, and if left unhealed, it plants seeds of insecurity, fear, and bitterness. But rejection is not the end of your story—it is often God's redirection. What man rejects God can redeem. The stone that the builders rejected became the chief cornerstone (Psalm 118:22). Rejection may feel like abandonment, but in God's hands it becomes the very stage where He reveals your true worth, calling, and destiny.

The Process of Renewal

Renewing the mind isn't instant—it's a daily discipline. Read the Word even when your emotions resist. The Word will never fail you. Speak truth over yourself when lies rise up. In order to continue on your process of renewal, don't allow what others say to affect your process. Keep speaking truth and keep speaking life. Also, take every thought captive as in 2 Corinthians 10:5:

"Casting down imaginations, and every high thing that exalteth itself against the knowledge of God, and bringing into captivity every thought to the obedience of Christ; and submit it to Christ."

By surrounding yourself with life-giving voices and not those familiar dysfunctional voices that will try to stop your process, you will find yourself breaking barriers that were built on dysfunction. Each life-giving voice acts as a reminder of who you are in Christ and who you are becoming. They speak truth where lies once lived, hope where despair tried to settle, and affirmation where rejection left scars. As those voices pour into you, they help you to silence the noise of doubt, shame, and fear. Soon, you realize that the walls built by dysfunction are not permanent prisons but temporary obstacles, and with the right voices guiding and praying over you, those walls come tumbling down.

Reject Shame and Replace with Grace

To walk in freedom, you must reject shame and replace it with grace. Shame chains you to your past, reminding you of every mistake and failure, while grace points you to the cross where every sin was already covered. Shame says, *"You are unworthy."* Grace declares, *"You are forgiven and redeemed."* Shame causes you to hide, but grace calls you out of hiding and clothes you with righteousness. When you choose grace over shame, you no longer see yourself through the lens of brokenness but through the eyes of God's love. Rejecting shame is not pretending your past doesn't exist—it's choosing to no longer let it define you. Grace gives you permission to heal, to grow, and to walk boldly into the future God has prepared for you.

To walk in true freedom, you must reject shame and replace it with grace. Shame is a heavy chain that keeps you tied to your past, whispering lies that you are unworthy, unlovable, or beyond repair. It magnifies your mistakes and minimizes your progress. Shame convinces you that you must hide from God and people, carrying the weight of guilt alone. But grace breaks that cycle. Grace points you back to the cross where every sin, every failure, and every shortcoming was already nailed and covered.

Shame says, *"You are defined by what you've done."* Grace declares, *"You are defined by what Christ has done for you."* Shame tries to silence your voice, but grace restores your confidence. Shame tries to disqualify you, but grace reminds you that God chooses the broken and makes them whole.

Replacing shame with grace does not mean ignoring your past; it means refusing to let it hold power over your future. Grace transforms your wounds into testimonies, your scars into reminders of survival, and your failures into stepping stones toward destiny. When you walk in grace, you can look at your past without fear and your future without shame.

Grace invites you to come boldly before the throne of God (Hebrews 4:16), to stand clothed not in your own righteousness but in His. Grace tells you that no mistake is final, no season is wasted, and no label of shame can stick to a redeemed child of God. Reject shame, embrace grace, and step forward with the confidence that you are forgiven, loved, and chosen.

This process doesn't just help you think better—it helps you live better. Your confidence begins to grow. Your self-talk becomes kind. You stop reacting in fear and start responding in faith.

New Mind, New Life

A renewed mind is a protected mind. It recognizes the lies of the enemy before they take root. It remembers who you are *and* Whose you are. It no longer defaults to survival—it chooses abundance, authority, and identity in Christ.

You're not who you used to be, so stop thinking like who you used to be. Let God rewire your thoughts and restore your mind. Because a renewed mind doesn't just break cycles—it prevents them from ever returning.

Declaration of Grace (read aloud and repeat)

I reject shame and I embrace grace. Shame has no authority over my life. My past does not define me—Christ does. I am forgiven. I am redeemed. I am chosen. I will no longer hide in guilt or fear, for I am clothed in righteousness through Jesus Christ. Every lie of shame is broken and every chain of condemnation is destroyed.

I walk in freedom, I walk in healing, and I walk in the unshakable love of God. From this day forward, I replace shame with grace—and I will never look back.

Prayer: Renewing the Mind

Gracious Father, Your Word declares in Romans 12:2 that I am not to conform to the pattern of this world but to be transformed by the renewing of my mind. So today, I surrender my thoughts to You—every lie I've believed, every false identity I've embraced, every fear that has shaped how I see myself.

God, I ask You to uproot the thoughts that don't belong. Uproot the belief that I'm not enough. Uproot the patterns of shame, guilt, and fear. Pull down every imagination and argument that exalts itself above Your truth. Help me to recognize the difference between my thoughts and Your thoughts and give me the strength to reject anything that does not align with Your Word.

Renew my mind, Lord—day by day, moment by moment. Teach me to think like someone who is free, not bound. To think like someone who is loved, not rejected. To think like someone who is chosen, not forgotten. Let my inner dialogue reflect Your heart and Your promises.

When the enemy whispers condemnation, help me to speak Your truth louder. When anxiety rises, anchor me in Your peace. When old patterns try to return, remind me that I am a new creation in Christ. As 2 Corinthians 5:17 says, *"Therefore if any man be in Christ, he is a new creature: old things are passed away; behold, all things are become new."*

I declare that my mind is being transformed. I no longer follow the pattern of dysfunction—I follow the pattern of heaven. I take every thought captive and make it obedient to Christ. I put on the mind of Christ and walk boldly in wisdom, peace, and clarity.

Let my renewed mind produce a renewed life. Let my thoughts reflect my freedom. Let my words build, not tear down. And let my mindset match the destiny You've designed for me.

In the name of Jesus—Amen.

Part IV
Life After the Break

CHAPTER 10

$\leftarrow \infty\!\ominus\!-(\!{\scriptstyle\circ}\!)\!-\!\infty\!\ominus \rightarrow$

THE FRUIT OF THE SHIFT

When a cycle breaks, something beautiful begins to grow. It may not be obvious at first, freedom often starts as a whisper before it becomes a roar—but over time, the evidence of healing becomes undeniable. God doesn't just break cycles to remove pain. He breaks them to make room for fruit—for the kind of life that reflects His goodness, peace, and power.

The fruit of the shift is unmistakable. It's not just in how loudly you praise but in how deeply you rest. It's in the boundaries you now uphold, the peace that governs your decisions, and the joy that no longer needs a reason. You're no longer reacting from your wounds—you're responding from your healing. The shift shows up in your conversations, your posture, and your prayers. You no longer beg for what you used to chase; you stand in confidence, knowing who you are and Whose you are. This fruit isn't surface-level—it's rooted. And it's the evidence that the cycle truly broke and something far greater took its place.

The Fruit of the Shift comes when you make the conscious decision to surrender old patterns and embrace the new life God is birthing in you. Shifts are not always easy; they stretch you, challenge you, and often pull you out of your comfort zone. But every shift brings fruit—peace where there was once chaos, clarity where there was once confusion, and purpose where there was once wandering. The fruit of the shift is growth, maturity, and a deeper intimacy with God. It is the evidence that you are no longer who you used to be. Just like a tree produces fruit in its season, the spiritual shift produces visible change in your life—your words, your actions, your relationships, and even the way you see yourself begin to align with God's truth. What once held you captive no longer has power because the shift has birthed new fruit that testifies to your transformation.

The Visible Signs of Change

You'll know the shift is taking root when:

- You no longer tolerate what once felt normal. Have you ever found yourself not laughing at the same jokes that you once thought were funny? If you have, this is a sign of change. Change doesn't mean that you stop—it means that you evolve. When you no longer tolerate bad behavior, deliverance has occurred.

- Peace becomes your default, not chaos. When staying home to read your Bible and watch a movie becomes the highlight of your day, you know there's a change in you. Protecting your peace becomes a big deal in your life and your number one goal. Something has just shifted in your life called change.

- Your "no" gets stronger and your "yes" becomes more intentional. No was a word that I couldn't say, no matter who it was. I would try to figure out a way to help or to do exactly what everyone wanted from me. One day, I finally said, "No, I can't do that for you." However, on the other hand, when I began to say, "Yes," to God, that's when my life began to change.

- Your relationships become healthier because *you're* healthier. My husband often says, "Thank you for saving me from myself!" But the reality is that if it had not been for God, who was on my side and brought about a change in me, I don't know how I would have been. Once I was able to walk in deliverance and freedom I was able to create a healthy relationship with my husband.

- You stop shrinking and start showing up fully. There comes a moment in healing where you no longer apologize for your presence. You stop shrinking to fit into the spaces that once tolerated your silence and you start showing up fully—as the healed, whole, and holy version of yourself. You stop minimizing your voice to make others comfortable and start walking in the authority God gave you.

- You parent differently. You love differently. You believe differently. When the cycle breaks, everything changes, including how you show up in the most intimate parts of your life. I parent differently, not from pain but from healing. I give my children what I didn't receive—consistency, affirmation, emotional safety, and grace. My children are my heart and for them to become healthy, I had first to become delivered.

You love differently, not from fear or need but from overflow. You stop chasing validation and start offering love that is whole, honest, and rooted in truth. And you believe differently. You no longer see God through the lens of trauma but through the clarity of relationship. Your faith is no longer just a ritual—it becomes a resting place. The shift isn't just seen in what you leave behind—it's proven in how you live now.

These aren't just random changes. This is spiritual fruit. The Bible says:

"By their fruit you will recognize them…"—Matthew 7:16

"The fruit of the Spirit is love, joy, peace, patience, kindness, goodness, faithfulness, gentleness, and self-control."—Galatians 5:22–23

When God breaks the cycle, His Spirit begins to bear fruit in places that were once barren. What once felt like a graveyard becomes a garden—life springs up where death used to reign. The bitterness that once ruled your heart is replaced with joy. The silence you grew up in is now filled with worship. The brokenness that ran through your bloodline is now met with healing that flows from the cross. God doesn't just remove the curse—He replaces it with purpose. He plants peace where there was once anxiety and hope where despair had taken root. This is the evidence of transformation: when your scars start producing fruit and your pain becomes someone else's pathway to healing.

Blessings Beyond You

The fruit of your shift doesn't stop with you. Your healing touches those around you. Your children feel it. Your spouse notices it.

Your friends begin to ask what changed. You become the evidence of what God can do with a surrendered life. And sometimes, the most powerful testimony isn't the pain you overcame—it's the peace you now walk in. The shift doesn't make you perfect. It makes you aware, anchored, and available to the fullness of God's promise.

Prayer: The Fruit of the Shift

Father God, Thank You for the shift You've started in me. Thank You for not just breaking cycles—but planting new seeds. I bless You not only for the battles You've brought me out of but for the new fruit I now see growing in my life—fruit that testifies to Your faithfulness, power, and grace.

I thank You for peace that now guards my heart and mind, where there used to be chaos.

I thank You for clarity, where confusion once clouded my decisions.

I thank You for joy, where depression once ruled.

I thank You for boundaries, where there used to be brokenness and people-pleasing.

I thank You for growth, even in seasons where I felt planted in pain.

Lord, I recognize that this fruit didn't come from my strength—it came from Your Spirit. You've done a deep work in me. You shifted my mindset. You reordered my steps. You gave me new language, new vision, new patterns, and new posture.

Help me to steward this shift with humility. Let me never forget who I used to be—so I can always praise You for who I'm becoming. Let the fruit in my life be evident to others—not for applause but for testimony. Let them see Your glory in my healing, Your hand in my decisions, and Your Spirit in my actions.

And Father, let this fruit not stop with me. Let it multiply. Let it flow to my family, my children, my community, and every life I touch. Let my shift spark a ripple of transformation in others.

I declare that what I'm seeing now is just the beginning. The shift is real. The fruit is proof. And You, Lord, get all the glory.

In Jesus' name, Amen.

CHAPTER 11

←⌇⌇(o)⌇⌇→

WALKING IN NEWNESS

Once the cycle breaks and the shift begins you step into something many people never experience, newness. Not just a new situation or new surroundings—but a new way of living, thinking, and being. This is more than a season change—this is a spiritual reset. It's a SPIRITUAL RESET!

Romans 6:4: *"Just as Christ was raised from the dead through the glory of the Father, we too may walk in newness of life."* Newness is not perfection—it's progress with God. It's a daily walk of choosing healing, choosing truth, choosing freedom—even when old patterns try to whisper you back into bondage.

Newness requires courage because you must step out of what is familiar, especially if what was familiar is broken. It calls you to walk by faith into an identity you've never fully lived before. Old cycles lose their grip when you refuse to entertain them. Each choice to trust God becomes a brick laid in the foundation of your new life.

Newness also brings responsibility. With every reset comes a fresh assignment, and with every fresh assignment comes the grace to fulfill it. You're no longer just surviving; you are stewarding the promise, carrying the testimony, and modeling freedom for those who are still bound. And while the world may try to remind you of who you were, heaven celebrates who you are becoming. That's the beauty of newness: it's not just about leaving the past behind—it's about embracing the future God has prepared.

We sing about walking in newness, but until we break the necessary strongholds and change, it's going to be impossible to walk in newness. Each new day granted by God is a great opportunity to walk in newness. One must make it in their minds that they will no longer settle for the things of the old. *Decree and declare that you will no longer allow the words that you speak not to correspond to the actions you take.* What you are saying is that you will no longer speak of newness while refusing to step out of the oldness.

Daily Choices Lead to Eternal Impact

Now that you have made the declaration over your life that you will walk in newness there are some things that you must adhere to as walking in newness means that you no longer define yourself by your past. Who you used to be can't compare to how God sees you in your present. A big part about deliverance is forgetting those things that are behind you and pressing forward to the things that await you.

Another choice you must make is to start measuring success by peace and not performance. You may not have a large following, you may not be famous, you may not be popular or the greatest influencer, but you have peace of mind. You are successful because you have peace. Too often, we seek performance over peace and think that we have become successful. Our daily choices will lead to our eternal impact. Once you have made a bold stance to choose the correct path, you will begin making decisions from a place of healing, not habit. What that means is that you will stop making decisions based on what you used to do or how you used to do it.

I choose newness because I want to walk with God—confidence, not insecurity. In ministry, the focus is meant to be on God's glory and the people you are called to serve. Insecurity can make you overly focused on yourself—your weaknesses, your image, and your fear of failure—rather than trusting that God equips those He calls. *"Not that we are competent in ourselves to claim anything for ourselves, but our competence comes from God."* 2 Corinthians 3:5. Each step you take in newness breaks the enemy's narrative and builds God's legacy in your life.

You are not who you used to be and you don't have to apologize for it. You are no longer the person who stayed silent. You're no longer stuck in survival mode. You don't shrink, settle, or self-abandon anymore. You walk tall—not in pride but in purpose. You can walk light, not because life is always easy but because you're no longer carrying what doesn't belong to you. You're walking in the newness of grace, identity, and healing. And this walk is only just beginning because the heaviness is lifted.

When the heaviness lifts, it feels as though a fog has finally cleared. The weight that once pressed on your chest, slowed your steps, and dimmed your joy is replaced with lightness, freedom, and peace. What seemed impossible to shake off becomes a testimony that God's presence truly breaks every chain. You can breathe deeper, smile wider, and move with renewed strength because the burden is no longer yours to carry. It has been surrendered, released, and exchanged for His perfect rest.

Prayer for Walking in Newness

Heavenly Father, I thank You for the gift of new life in Christ. Your Word declares that if anyone is in Christ, they are a new creation; old things have passed away, and all things have become new. Today, I choose to walk in that newness. Lord, help me to release every old pattern, every broken cycle, and every weight that tries to hold me back. Wash my mind with Your truth, renew my spirit with Your presence, and align my steps with Your will.

As I walk in newness, let my words bring life, let my thoughts reflect Your peace, and let my actions demonstrate Your love. Remind me daily that newness is not perfection, but progress—progress that comes by walking closely with You. I declare by faith that I am no longer bound by what was; I am free to step into what You are doing now. I embrace this season of transformation, healing, and breakthrough. May my life be a testimony to Your grace and a light for others to see.

In Jesus' name, Amen.

CHAPTER 12

$\leftarrow \text{℩℩-(o)-℩℩} \rightarrow$

BECOMING THE TESTIMONY

A t some point in your healing journey, you'll realize something profound—that you're no longer just telling the story, you have *become* the story. You've become the living, breathing evidence of what God can do when someone refuses to repeat what broke them. Your life is no longer just about what you came through. It's about who you've become—and *who God is through you.*

Your life is the undeniable proof of God's power, grace, and faithfulness. Every time you overcame what should have broken you, every step you took after the storm, and every smile you found in the midst of pain tells the story of His hand on you. You don't have to defend your calling or explain your transformation; your very existence, your progress, your resilience is the evidence. When people look at you, they see that cycles can be broken, healing is possible, and newness is real. Your life is the proof that God still redeems, restores, and makes all things new.

People may never read a Bible, but they'll read your life. They'll notice your peace. Your boundaries. Your growth. They'll see how you no longer tolerate what once defined you.

They'll hear the strength in your "yes" and the healing in your "no." You won't need to convince anyone of your transformation. The fruit speaks for itself. *"And they overcame him by the blood of the Lamb and the word of their testimony..."* —Revelation 12:11

Your story, the part you used to hide—is now your weapon. Your testimony tears down shame, awakens others to hope, and shows that cycles don't have to continue.

You Are Someone Else's Breakthrough

Do you believe that you are someone else's breakthrough? The enemy wanted you to keep silent; however, God wants to use your voice to help bring others out. Every healed wound becomes a roadmap for someone else. Think about that for one moment. You had to go through hurt and pain just for someone else to be free. Every cycle you break creates a path for someone behind you. You become the mentor, *the intercessor*, the encourager, the cycle-breaker others were praying for. You are what someone else needs to believe: *If God did it for them, He can do it for me.*

Becoming the testimony means your life becomes a legacy. A living witness that the blood of Jesus is still breaking chains. A declaration that healing is real. That wholeness is possible. That the cycle is not just broken, it becomes unalive and buried. The struggle is broken; your healing is here. You are not just the product of what happened. You are the prophecy fulfilled. The answer to a generational prayer. You are the cycle breaker, generational curse dismantler, and the living testimony of God, the only One who made all things new.

God often works through people to bring answers to prayer, healing, and hope. Just as Moses became Israel's breakthrough from Egypt and Esther became the breakthrough for her people, your obedience and faith can open doors for others. Your testimony, your encouragement, or even a simple act of kindness may be the very thing God uses to lift someone out of despair. The struggles you have overcome were not only for you—they prepared you to strengthen someone else. When you walk in love, prayer, and obedience, you carry the power to become the answer to another person's cry, showing that God truly uses His children to bless one another. You are someone else's breakthrough.

Part V
Prayer Will
Change You

Chapter 13

←⌇⌇(◦)⌇⌇→

I Am An Intercessor!

I have been chosen by God to stand in the gap, to lift up the broken, the weary, and the lost before His throne of grace. I carry burdens that are not my own, yet I trust the Spirit of God to strengthen me for the assignment. My prayers shift atmospheres, intercept attacks, and open doors that no man can shut. I wage war not in the flesh but in the Spirit, pulling down strongholds and releasing heaven's agenda on Earth.

I do not pray for recognition; I pray for results. My voice may be hidden, but my prayers echo in heaven. I am a watchman on the wall, alert and ready to sound the alarm. I am a spiritual warrior, clothed in the armor of God, interceding with power, persistence, and faith. I am a bridge of mercy between God and His people, an advocate for the hurting, a midwife for destinies yet unborn.

I will not faint in prayer, for I know the fervent, effectual prayers of the righteous avail much. James 5:16: *"Confess your faults one to another, and pray one for another, that ye may be healed. The effectual fervent prayer of a righteous man availeth much."* I will stand when others fall, I will cry out when others are silent, and I will carry the burdens of others until breakthrough comes. I am marked; I am chosen; I am appointed for this very work. I am an intercessor—called, anointed, and equipped by God. This is my identity, this is my assignment, and this is my declaration.

Understanding the Assignment

So many times in my life I could not understand why I was always being asked to pray for someone. There were moments when I desperately needed someone to pray for me, yet I found myself constantly praying for others. It wasn't until I truly realized what it meant to be an intercessor that I began to see more clearly.

When I was younger, I would hear the mothers in the church say, "You'll understand it better by and by." Well, by and by, I did begin to understand. I grew up in the country, where the only thing we did was go to church—what felt like seven days a week. As a child, it seemed that if we weren't in school, we were in church. At that age, your purpose is not clear and you don't yet understand the will of God for your life. But one thing is certain: even when you don't fully understand your assignment, if your foundation is set in Him, you have no choice but to build on it.

I remember taking my husband to his first NFL game. I went with the intention of just enjoying the experience. But while sitting there, the Lord spoke to me about what it truly means to be an intercessor. I watched the team work together—one side pressing against the other, the quarterback trying to connect with his teammates, while the opposing team worked just as hard to disrupt the connection. That's when the Lord showed me: this is the struggle of intercession.

Sometimes, you are connected to people and situations in ways God never intended and the opposition you see isn't always your enemy—it can also be your assignment. Intercessors step in to *intercept* what the enemy intended for someone else. Just like when a football is intercepted, the target changes hands—you carry what was meant for another. That's the weight of intercession.

The Call of an Intercessor

Many people say they are intercessors, but true intercession is not about our opinions or preferences. Intercessors must have discernment, but they also must lay down judgment. To intercede is to pray, to petition, and to intervene on behalf of someone else. It means you willingly take on the struggle so that someone else might have relief.

The moment I fully embraced praying for others, the struggle in my own life intensified. That's the mark of a true intercessor: when you carry burdens that were never yours but you hold them until God brings breakthrough.

When an intercessor prays, things shift in the unseen realm. Heaven leans in. Hell trembles. And lives are preserved that may have otherwise been destroyed. Intercession is not casual prayer—it is standing in the gap between God and His people, between the attack and the victim, between life and death.

Ezekiel 22:30 says, *"I looked for someone among them who would build up the wall and stand before me in the gap on behalf of the land so I would not have to destroy it, but I found no one."* An intercessor is that "someone." When we pray, we become the wall of protection and the bridge of mercy at the same time.

When an intercessor prays, the burden is often heavy. Sometimes you will wake up in the middle of the night with someone on your heart, not even knowing what they are going through. Other times, you may suddenly feel sorrow, uneasiness, or even urgency without explanation. That is the Spirit's signal—He is placing an assignment in your spirit.

This is where many struggle because carrying another's burden is not easy. Yet Galatians 6:2 reminds us, *"Carry each other's burdens, and in this way you will fulfill the law of Christ."* Intercessors are carriers and prayer is how we deliver what we carry to the throne room of God.

There was a time when I could not sleep for three nights straight. I kept hearing a young woman's name in my spirit. I didn't know her situation, but I obeyed and prayed. Days later, I learned she had been battling depression and had considered taking her life. While I prayed, she felt a sudden peace wash over her. That is the unseen power of intercession—it can literally save lives. When an intercessor prays, what the enemy meant for harm is intercepted. Just like in a football game where an interception changes the entire direction of the play, prayer shifts the outcome.

Abraham interceded for Lot and his prayers preserved a remnant from destruction.

Moses interceded for Israel and his prayer turned away God's wrath.

Hannah interceded for a child and her tears brought forth Samuel, who became a prophet to the nations.

These were not shallow prayers; they were deep cries of the heart. Intercession taps into the heart of God until His will is birthed on Earth. The people you are assigned to intercede for may not even know you are the reason their life is still intact. You may never be thanked, but heaven keeps record. When an intercessor prays, it is not about being seen or heard by people. The ministry of intercession is hidden. You may labor for hours in prayer and the very ones you intercede for might never acknowledge you. But intercession isn't about recognition—it's about results. Romans 8:34 reminds us that *"Christ Jesus … is at the right hand of God and is also interceding for us."* Even now, Jesus intercedes silently for His people. When we intercede, we partner with His priestly work.

I once prayed for a co-worker who never knew I was interceding for her. She was dealing with family struggles and health battles. Months later, she testified how she almost gave up but felt "someone was praying." That's when I realized: intercession isn't about us— it's about being a hidden vessel for God's will to flow through. Sometimes we make the mistake of calling people to let them know that we are praying for them, instead of praying and interceding. God has given you instructions to pray and that doesn't require you to reach out for recognition. God said PRAY so that you can block what's coming. You have been called to break cycles in another person's life. There is a reward for your obedience. When an intercessor prays, heaven responds. Sometimes the answer comes quickly; other times it takes years. But obedience is never wasted. The greatest reward of an intercessor is not applause but partnership with God. Your prayers leave a mark on eternity. The doors you open in prayer may bless generations long after you are gone.

When an Intercessor Prays...

- Cycles are broken.
- Chains are destroyed.
- Strongholds collapse.
- Generational curses are cut off.
- Healing is released.
- Destinies are preserved.
- Families are restored.

This is the invisible, yet undeniable, work of an intercessor.

Praying for the Intercessor

Heavenly Father, I thank You for calling me as an intercessor. I may not always understand the weight of this assignment, but I know You trust me to stand in the gap. Lord, place on my heart those You want me to pray for. Teach me to carry their burdens to You and not in my own strength.

Today, I lift up every intercessor. I pray for Your protection, Your healing, and Your deliverance in their lives. I cancel every plan of the enemy that seeks to harm them. I ask that Your will be done and Your kingdom come in their lives.

Lord, strengthen me for this calling. Let me not grow weary in prayer. Remind me that my labor in intercession is not in vain. Use me as a vessel of mercy, a wall of protection, and a bridge of grace. In Jesus' name, Amen.

CONCLUSION

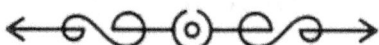

THE CYCLE THAT STAYS BROKEN

You didn't just survive. You didn't just recover. You broke the cycle—and by God's grace, it will stay broken. This book began with patterns, pain, and silence, but it ends with purpose, power, and legacy. You are no longer living under the weight of what was. You are walking in the freedom of what *is* and the promise of what's still to come.

What's broken can't bind you again. The cycle didn't end because you were the strongest.

It ended because you were willing. In every battle, you must be willing to confront the truth.

You must be willing to heal and be willing to let God in. Although it's not easy, you must be willing to do what no one else had the courage or capacity to do. And because of that, you are the pivot point. The shift. The turning. The answered prayer that changed everything.

There will be days when old patterns try to resurface. There will be moments when you question your progress. But hear this: *Freedom is a journey, not a moment.* The cycle broke the day you decided to stop living beneath your inheritance and you never have to go back. Let your life remain a loud declaration: "I am free. I am whole. I am healed. And it stops with me." You are the cycle breaker. And because of you, the cycle stays broken.

Deliverance Prayer: Breaking Every Cycle

Father God, In the name of Jesus, I come boldly before Your throne of grace. I surrender every cycle, every stronghold, and every generational burden that has followed my life. Lord, I acknowledge that some of these patterns were inherited, some were learned, and some were chosen in my brokenness—but today, I choose freedom.

I renounce every lie I believed about myself, my worth, and my identity. I break agreement with the voices of fear, shame, rejection, pride, perversion, addiction, anger, and abandonment. I silence every voice that is not Yours. I cancel every demonic assignment that has tried to operate in my life through trauma, curses, soul ties, and rebellion.

In the name of Jesus, I break every generational curse—spoken or unspoken, known or unknown. I sever every root of bitterness, every legacy of dysfunction, and every hidden sin that has tried to pass through my bloodline. I plead the blood of Jesus over my life, my mind, my heart, my family, and every future generation.

Lord, I receive Your healing and I allow Your truth to uproot every lie. I declare that I am not bound by the past. I am not defined by the trauma. I am not who the enemy says I am; I am who You say I am—whole, redeemed, restored, and loved.

I speak to every cycle and command it to break now in Jesus' name. Where there was chaos let there be peace. Where there was silence let there be truth. Where there was bondage let there be breakthrough. Where there was pain let purpose arise.

Father, build in me what the enemy tried to destroy. Plant Your Spirit deep within me. Fill every empty space with Your presence. Let Your Word be my anchor, Your Spirit my guide, and Your love my covering.

Today, I closed every door that was opened to the enemy, knowingly or unknowingly. I walk in the authority You've given me as a child of God. I declare that the cycle is broken, the stronghold is dismantled, and the curse is canceled—permanently.

In the mighty name of Jesus, I am free. Amen.

A Note to My Spiritual Mother, Rev. Dr. Lavern Runell Washington

A Mother Beyond Blood

Dr. Washington, whom I affectionately called "MOM," was more to me than a Spiritual Mother. We know that spiritual mothers are not chosen by chance but appointed by God. She saw beyond my flaws, prayed for me through storms, and nurtured the call of God within me. My spiritual mother was more than a mentor; she was a covering, a teacher, and a vessel of wisdom who helped shape me into who I am today.

A life that taught and touched me through the years. If you knew her, you would know that her life was a sermon all on its own. She walked in humility, clothed herself in compassion, and carried wisdom that could only come from spending time with God. She didn't just tell me how to live right; she showed me through her daily walk. Her faith was unshakable, her counsel steady, and her love for God undeniable. There were countless moments when her prayers became my lifeline. She interceded when I was too weak to pray for myself. Her words pierced the heavens and pulled down strength when I needed it most. She reminded me that prayer isn't just communication with God—it is a weapon, a shield, and a way of life.

I will never forget that when I wanted to give up, she wouldn't allow it. We would sit up for hours and talk. We would go to her favorite restaurant and eat crabs for hours, laughing, crying, praying, and eating the entire time. I thank God for favoring me by giving me someone who looked at me as if I were the one she had birthed. She could chastise me and show me love at the same time. She wouldn't allow me to feel sorry for myself. When I was mad and emotional, she would say, "God doesn't care about your emotions—He cares about your obedience." She wouldn't allow me to stay in that place.

Her legacy lives on in me and so many others that she has touched. Although she is no longer here in body, her legacy continues in every lesson, every scripture, and every prayer she deposited into my life. I carry her teachings as a mantle, determined to honor her by living out the very principles she instilled in me: faithfulness, obedience, integrity, and love. Dad, Rev. Bernard Washington, is carrying the torch on Wash Lives Ministry Bible Line. He is so strong, Mom. You would be so proud of him. He has some good days and some bad days, but through it all, he is moving forward just as you would want him to.

The Apostle Paul said, *"Imitate me as I imitate Christ"* (1 Corinthians 11:1). My spiritual mother lived this truth. By following her example, I gained a spiritual inheritance that cannot be measured in earthly terms. I rise stronger, pray harder, and love deeper because of her.

To my spiritual mother: Thank you for seeing me, for covering me, and for loving me as your own. Thank you for every prayer, every correction, and every encouragement. Though you have gone on to glory, your voice, your teachings, and your spirit live on in me. Your memory will forever be a blessing and your legacy will continue to live on through the lives of those you have touched in church and on the Bible Line. I really miss you. Keep watching over us. I love you.

Continue to rest, Mom!

Dr. Natasha Bibbins Bio

Dr. Natasha Bibbins is a God-fearing woman devoted to her faith, her family, and her divine calling. She is a loving wife, mother, prophet, pastor, co-author, author, certified life and executive leadership coach, sister, and friend. Natasha is the founder of several impactful ministries and nonprofit organizations, including Natasha Bibbins Ministries, Forever Fire Empowerment (501c3), Sisters Empowering Sisters Ministries, The Recharge Movement (501c3), and Recharge Outreach Ministry.

She is also the visionary behind The Walker Family Prayer Call, reflecting her deep belief in the biblical principle that family is one's first ministry, as rooted in 1 Timothy 3:5: *"If anyone does not know how to manage his own family, how can he take care of God's church?"*

Natasha became a best-selling co-author for *Dreamer on the Rise* (2020) and again with *Called to Intercede* (2022). She is also the best-selling author and visionary of *God Will Right Your Wrong Too* (2024) and *I Almost Gave Up* (2025), co-written with other inspiring authors. Additionally, she has written the transformative *Recharge Empowerment Journal* (2022) and is one of the authors of *God Will Right Your Wrong* (2023), for all of which she is the visionary.

In January 2023, Natasha was awarded an Honorary Doctorate in Christian Leadership from the School of the Great Commission Theological Seminary. Academically, she holds a Master's degree in Management, a Bachelor's in Business Management, and an Associate degree in Business Administration. While working on her Doctor of Strategic Leadership at Liberty University, she earned a Ph.D. in Christian Leadership and Business from Chosen Christian

University in 2025. Additionally, she earned a second Master's degree in Public Administration from Old Dominion University in 2025.

Her leadership has been recognized with multiple honors, including the Servant Leader Award and the Walking in Grace Leadership Award, both of which she received in 2022. She also received a "Kingdom Builder" award in 2025.

Natasha is joyfully married to Pastor Michael Bibbins and is the proud mother of Wilniqua and William Battle as well as three bonus children: Michael II, Shenelle, and Pamela. She is also blessed with a granddaughter, Aniya, and a son-in-law, Harold.

Her favorite scripture, Romans 8:18, fuels her perseverance: *"For I reckon that the sufferings of this present time are not worthy to be compared with the glory which shall be revealed in us."* It serves as her constant reminder to press forward—because greatness is always just around the corner.

Follow Dr. Natasha Bibbins
Facebook: DrNatasha Bibbins
Instagram: Dr.Natasha Bibbins
Clubhouse: DrNatasha Bibbins
YouTube: DrNatasha Bibbins
Website: www.natashabibbins.com
Email: admin@natashabibbins.com
Ministry Phone: 757-652-2245